CLAN
MACPHERSON

Extensively Revised

COMPILED BY
Alan McNie

CASCADE PUBLISHING COMPANY
Jedburgh, Scotland

Genealogical Research:
Research regrettably cannot be undertaken by the publisher. A non-profit organisation, The Scots Ancestry Research Society, 3 Albany Street, Edinburgh, undertake research for an agreed fee.

Alan McNie, 1983, extensively revised, 1989
©Cascade Publishing Company
Rowandene, Belses, Jedburgh, Scotland

ISBN 0 907614 11 6

Page 1 Explanation:

The illustrated tartan is the Modern MacPherson. The motto on the crest badge means, 'Touch not the cat without a glove'. In the artist's montage the clan museum at Newtonmore is shown. Also depicted in the left foreground are two items of clan memorabilia at the museum: Jamie Macpherson's Fiddle and the Black Chanter, traditionally linked with the Battle of North Inch in 1396. Also illustrated in the foreground is the clan plant badge, white heather.

MACPHERSON

TOUCH·NOT·THE·CAT·BOT·A·GLOVE·

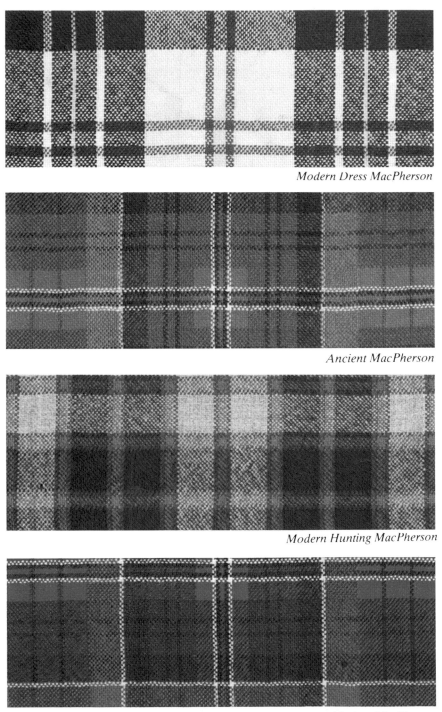

Modern Dress MacPherson

Ancient MacPherson

Modern Hunting MacPherson

Modern MacPherson

MacPherson Country

The map used below and on the following page is intended basically as a pictorial reference. It is accurate enough, however, to be correlated with a current map. The clan boundaries are only marginally correct. No precise boundaries were kept in early times and territories were fluctuating frequently.

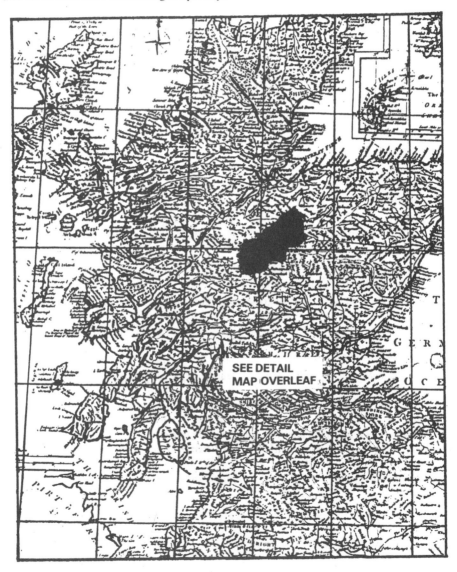

MacPherson
CLAN MAP

1. Ballindalloch A Macpherson inherited this estate in 1806

2. Cluny Castle Former clan seat − now private residence

3. Culloden Macphersons arrived too late to support Jacobite cause

4. Invereshie One of the oldest cadet branches

5. Kingussie Origin of the clan name

6. Loch Ericht Ewan Macpherson of Cluny stayed in concealment for nine years after Jacobite rebellion

7. Monadhliath Range Separated Macpherson territory from Mackintosh property

8. Newtonmore Home of Clan Macpherson Museum

9. Ruthven Castle Defended by the Macphersons during the Huntly rebellion of 1594

Cairngorm *Northern extremity of Macpherson territory*

CLAN
MACPHERSON

Condensed from Highland Clans of Scotland
George Eyre-Todd, 1923

Great has been the discussion, since ever an interest came to be taken in these things regarding the origin of the famous Clan Chattan. Eager to derive the clan from an antiquity as remote as possible, its historians have claimed that it represents the early Cati of Gaul mentioned by Tacitus. They aver that this tribe, driven from its native lands by the Romans, settled in the remote north of Scotland, to which it gave the name of Cattiness or Caithness. Fantastic stories are told also of early settlers who took possession of a district in the north formerly infested by dangerous numbers of wild cats, which the new settlers destroyed. Another derivation of the name is from *cat* or *catti,* a weapon, and still another from Catav − Gaelic, *cad,* high, and *tobh,* a side, the high land of the Ord of Caithness. But the most probable appears to be the theory of tradition which derives the name simply from Gillecattan Mhor, "the big servant of St Katan," who appears as a fairly authentic personage of the time of Malcolm Canmore, and whose ancestor, according to tradition, was one of the Gaelic settlers who came over from Ireland to Scotland in those early centuries. The elder line, descended from this Gilliecatan Mhor, came to and end in the person of an only daughter named Eva, who in 1291 married Angus, the young chief of the MacIntoshes. This individual received from his father-in-law not only part of the old Clan Chattan lands of Glenlui and Loch Arkaig, but also, it is said, an investiture as chief of Clan Chattan itself. There was, however, it appears, a younger male line descended from Gilliecattan Mhor. The representative of this younger line in the twelfth century was a certain Muirich, priest or parson of the Culdee church at Kingussie. The priests of this church were not bound to celibacy. Indeed one of the reasons for the introduction of the Roman Church at that time was the abuse of the office by the Culdee priests, who were accused of alienating the church land in favour of their own families. The Macphersons are said to be descended from Kenneth, son of Ewen Baan, second of the five sons of this Muirich, from whom they take their names of macmhurich, son of Muirich, or Macpherson, son of the parson. It is through this descent that the Macphersons claim to be chiefs of the old Clan Chattan, declaring that it was not in the power of a Highland chief to transfer the chiefship through a daughter to another family.

The Macphersons are said to have acquired their possessions in Badenoch from King Robert the Bruce as a reward for certain services in expelling the Comyns from that district, but it is also possible that they had retained possession of some of the lands of the old Culdee Church of which their ancestor Muirich had been parson there. They emerge into history as a body of considerable strength in 1370 or 1386. In one or other of these years, the Camerons, who had retained actual possession of the old Clan Chattan lands of Glenlui or Loch Arkaig in despite of the Mackintosh lands in Strath nairn, and were returning home through Badenoch,when they were overtaken by Mackintosh, supported by his relatives, the chiefs of the Macphersons and the Davidsons.

The fact that Mackintosh was in command has been claimed by his clansmen to prove that he was recognised by the Macphersons and Davidsons as Chief of Clan Chattan. But the fact that the personal quarrel was his might sufficiently account for his leadership there, and it is significant that both the macphersons and the Davidsons found occasion to assert the seniority of their descent on the spot. The question arising as to who should have the place of honour on the right flank, the Macpherson chief claimed it as chief of the old Clan Chattan, and the Davidson chief claimed it as head of the senior cadet

Loch Arkaig

Mary Queen of Scots

branch of that clan. Mackintosh assigned the post to the Davidsons, and as a result the Macphersons straightaway withdrew their assistance. In the battle which followed at Invernahavon, Mackintosh, thus weakened, suffered defeat. There is a tradition that he then sent to the macpherson camp a minstrel who taunted these clansmen with cowardice, and that, enraged in consequence, they flew to arms, attacked the Camerons, and completely routed them.

According to some it was the difference between the different septs of Clan Chattan at Invernahavon which directly led to the famous fight of the "Threttie against Threttie" before King Robert III on the North Inch of Perth in 1396. Some assert that the clansmen arrayed against each other in that fight were the Macphersons and the Davidsons, but it seems more likely that the battle really was between the mackintoshes and the Camerons.

That the Macphersons remained of consequence in Badenoch is shown by entries in the Exchequer Rolls, which refer to supplies received by James II from Hugh Macpherson at Ruthven in that district in 1459. According to family tradition the chief, Ewen macpherson, was a staunch supporter of Queen Mary, while his son Andrew Macpherson and his clan certainly took part in the battle of Glenlivet in 1594, after defending the Earl of Huntly's castle of Ruthven successfully against the young Earl of Argyll, commanding the invading forces of King James VI.

During the events which led up to the battle of Glenlivet, and at the battle itself, the chief of the Mackintoshes was ranged with his clan on the side of the Earl of Moray and the King, while Macpherson with his men were on the side of the Earl of Huntly. Andrew Macpherson, the young chief, was at that time only tenant of Cluny, which property then belonged to the Earl of Huntly, and on 16th May, 1591, Huntly had obtained from him and nine of the chief men of his clan a bond securing their support. These circumstances may be taken as illustrative of the rivalry which appears always to have existed between the two great branches of Clan Chattan.

In the civil war of Charles I's time the Macphersons played a gallant part on the side of the King. From the register of the provincial synod of Moray it appears that Dougal Macpherson acted as Captain of Ruthven Castle, and that Ewen Macpherson of Cluny had joined

Marquis of Montrose

with Alastair Macdonald, the Marquess of Huntly, and the Great Marquess of Montrose in their daring military enterprise; that he had been present at the battles of Tibbermuir and Aberdeen, in which he had been in command of all the loyal forces of Badenoch. It was during one of the headlong attacks of this campaign, when the little Royalist forces were about to engage a party of the Covenanting Horse, that an incident occurred which is related effectively by Sir Walter Scott. A gentleman of Clan Macpherson was noticed to be crouching somewhat in the rear, and Macpherson of Nuid, taking the action to be one of cowardice, ran up to him and indignantly upbraided him with setting so bad an example. The clansman, however, answered, "I have only been fastening a spur to the heel of my brogue, for I mean in a few minutes to be mounted on one of these horses". And in a few minutes, sure enough he had fulfilled his intention.

It was shortly after this that the dispute between the heads of the Mackintoshes and Macphersons as to the chiefship of Clan Chattan found its way into a court of law. It was true that in 1609 Andrew Macpherson in Cluny had, with several other Macphersons, subscribed a bond of manrent, undertaking to maintain and defend the Chief of Mackintosh, "as it was of old according to the King of Scotland his gift of chieftainrie of the said Clan Chattan granted thereupon, in the which they are, and is abstricted to serve Mackintosh as their captain and chief." But such bonds were common instruments of the feudal centuries for temporary purposes, and did not necessarily mean the admission of a hereditary right. On the opposite side, in 1665, when the Mackintosh chief was preparing an expedition to assert his rights to the lands of Glenlui and Loch Arkaig against the Camerons, he asked the help of the Macphersons, and to prevent their action being construed into an admission that he was their chief, he executed a notarial deed declaring that they did so merely of their own good will and pleasure, and added on his own part, "I bind and oblige myself and friends and followers to assist, fortify, and join with the said Andrew, Lachlan, and John Macpherson, all their lawful and necessary adoes, being thereunto required." The trouble with the Camerons having, however, been settled, Mackintosh proceeded again to assert his chiefship of Clan Chattan, including the Macphersons. Once already the dispute between the rival chiefs had been on the point of

Loch-an-Eilean *Bordering northern clan holding*

an appeal to arms. In 1660 Mackintosh had begun to erect a mill, which was likely to injure one belonging to Macpherson of Cluny lower on the same stream. The fiery cross was sent through the Macpherson country, and Clan Vurich rushed to arms, stimulted by a traditional prophecy that at this time a great battle should be fought between the rival clans. The Mackintoshes and Macphersons faced each other at the site of the proposed mill. There Mackintosh, finding himself inferior in numbers, sent for help, first to the chief of the Grants and afterwards to the chief of the Farquharsons, but both of these chiefs refused to take arms against their neighbour Macpherson. In the end Mackintosh drew off his men, the Macphersons demolished the half-built mill, and its erection was finally abandoned.

In 1672, to end the dispute, Duncan Macpherson of Cluny applied for and obtained from the Lord Lyon the matriculation of arms as "the laird of Cluny Macpherson and the only and true representer of the ancient and honourable family of Clan Chattan." He proceeded, however, to carry the assertion of his rights too far. The Lyon Office had admitted him to be Chief of Clan Chattan. He now undertook under an order of the Privy Council to be responsible for the good behaviour of all the holders of his name; then, to protect himself, issued a requisition to landownders of his name in Badenoch to give him letters of relief undertaking to answer to him for the good behaviour of themselves and their own people. These gentlemen, not being his feudal vassals, naturally resented the assumption of feudal authority, and appealed against it to the Privy Council, and that body thereupon released him from his bond of cautionary and required him only to become responsible for his own tenants and servants and the persons of his name descended from his family, while the Laird of Mackintosh was required to become responsible, among others, for such of the name of Macpherson as might be his feudal vassals.. Further, at the instance of the Laird of Mackintosh, the Lord Lyon withdrew Cluny's previous matriculation of arms, and granted him a coat as a cadet of the Mackintoshes. The right to use supporters, the heraldic sign of chiefship, was also denied him, and it was not till 1873 that this right was conceded by the Lyon Office, the person to whom it was conceded being the late Ewen Macpherson of Cluny, who succeeded in 1817 and died in 1885.

Meanwhile the Macpherson chiefs paid little attention to the ruling of the Lord Lyon. In 1673 Cluny signed a contract of friendship with Macdonald of Glengarry "for himself and taken burden upon him for the haell name of Macpherson and some others called Old Clanchatten as cheefe and principall man thereof." It is true that in 1724, on consideration of receiving from the Mackintosh chief certain lands about Loch Laggan, the chief of the Macphersons signed an agreement renouncing in favour of Mackintosh all claim to be chief of Clan Chattan; but this deed is open to the suggestion that it refers only to the more modern Clan Chattan confederacy, which originated with the heiress Eva and Angus Mackintosh in 1291. There can be little doubt that if the descent from Muirich, parson of Kingussie, is authentic, Macpherson of Cluny is the actual heir-male of the older Clan Chattan chiefs, and since the battle of Invernahavon the existence of a chiefship of the Macphersons can never really have been in doubt.

It was the chief, Duncan Macpherson, who had the transactions with the Lord Lyon, who in 1680 at last procured from the Marquess of Huntly the permanent ownershp of Cluny, which had been possessed by his ancestors only as removable tenants. At the revolution in 1689, when Viscount Dundee opened his campaign in Scotland for King James, Cluny Macpherson was commissioned by the Estates to call together all the friends, kinsmen, vassals, and tenants under his command or influence, and reduce them into troops, companies, or a regiment, with power to name his inferior officers. Upon his death without male descendants in 1722 the representation passed to Lachlan Macpherson of Nuid, and it was he who signed the deed of 1724 above mentioned. In 1704 he married Jean, daughter of the famous Sir Ewen Cameron of Lochiel, and from this pair the later Cluny Macphersons have descended.

Lachlan Macpherson of Cluny lived till 1746, but it was his eldest son Ewen who figured so conspicuously as the Cluny Macpherson of the Jacobite rebellion of 1745. Only a short time previously had occurred the tragic incident of the Black Watch, which is one of the most pathetic in Scottish military history. The regiment, which had been enrolled to keep order in the Highlands, was marched to London, and a rumour spread that, contrary to its terms of enlistment, it was to be sent abroad. Suddenly and secretly the whole body set off for

Loch Laggan

Bonnie Prince Charlie

the north, but they were intercepted in Northamptonshire and marched back to the Tower. After trial many of them were banished to the Colonies, and three were shot, of whom two were Macphersons. This event had produced a strong feeling among the clansmen against the Government of King George. Before the landing of Prince Charles Edward, Cluny Macpherson had been granted a commission in Lord Loudon's regiment, but at the outbreak of the rebellion in 1745 he was captured by the Jacobites, and, shortly after the battle of Prestonpans, threw in his lot on the side of the Stewarts. With a hundred and twenty Macphersons he took part in the march to Derby, and at Clifton, during the retreat, it was he and his men who bore the chief brunt of the Hanoverian attack. During the winter Macpherson and his clan were allowed by the Prince to remain at home, and they were only on their way to rejoin the Prince's army when at Dalmagerry, near Moy, they were met by news of the defeat at Culloden. Had Cluny with his six hundred men reached the field in time it may well be believed they might have changed the fortunes of that day. As it was, the issue meant ruin for the chief. In the months which ensued his seat at Cluny was burned and his estate was forfeited. For some months he lived with his cousin, the younger Lochiel, in the famous hiding-place known as the cage on Ben Alder, where for a time he afforded shelter to the hunted Prince himself; and when Charles finally left for France he confided his military chest to the chief, and gave him a letter acknowledging his services and promising reward. For nine years Macpherson lived in caves and other hiding-places among his own people, whose affection for him may be judged by the fact that none was ever tempted by the Government reward to betray him. During these years, in 1750, his wife, a daughter of the notorious Simon, Lord Lovat, gave birth to his son and heir in a kiln for drying corn. When at last Macpherson escaped to France in 1755 he carried with him the Prince's military chest containing a considerable sum of money, which he had preserved intact, and his name remains among the most highly honoured of those who took part in the unfortunate Jacobite cause.

Duncan Macpherson, the chief born in the corn kiln, became Colonel of the 3rd Regiment of Foot Guards, and the forfeited estates were restored to him in 1784. He married Catherine, daughter of Sir

Ewen Cameron of Fassifern, another famous Jacobite, and died in 1817. His son Ewen was made a Companion of the Bath in 1881. He died in 1885, having been chief of the Macphersons for sixty-eight years, and the representation of the family has since been held in succession by his three sons, Duncan, Ewen, and Albert, the last of whom is the present chief.

Cluny Castle, Macpherson's seat, is a handsome modern building a few miles south-west of Kingussie. Its chief treasures are several highly interesting relics of the clan and of Prince Charles Edward Stewart. Among these last is the Prince's target, lined with leopard skin and richly and beautifully mounted with silver trophies and ornaments. These are also the Prince's gold-inlaid pistols, and silver-mounted sealskin sporran, as well as his lace ruffles given to Cameron of Fassifern, the farewell autography letter already mentioned, and a plate from which it was intended to print notes for the use of the Jacobite army. Another relic is the Bratach-uaine, or green banner of the clan, regarding which an old woman is said to have told the Duke of Cumberland that if he awaited its arrival he would certainly meet defeat. The Crios Breac, again, is a leathery belt of red morocco with silver studs representing the Angus Dei and head of St. John alternately, and believed to have been brought from the Holy Land by one of the early chiefs. But perhaps the chief treasure of the house is the Feadun Dhu or Black Chanter of Clan Chattan, which is said to have fallen from heaven to supply the loss of the chanter used by the piper who played in the famous battle of the "Threttie against Threttie" on the North Inch in 1396, and on the preservation of which the prosperity of the house of Cluny is believed by every true clansman to depend.

Ed. Note: Cluny Castle was purchased privately during the Second World War. Of the items mentioned in the preceding paragraph The Clan Macpherson Museum at Kingussie has six plates designed for printing notes, which were intended for use by the Jacobite army as mentioned. Also in the museum's possession is a copy of the original green banner. As well the museum has on display the famous Black Chanter from Cluny Castle.

Of other famous members of the Clan, two have been noted for their connection with Indian affairs. Sir John Macpherson, Bart., began life as a writer in the service of the East India Company at Madras in 1770, was dismissed for his conduct on a secret mission

Clan Macpherson Museum *Newtonmore*

James Macpherson
1736-1796

to this country for the Nabob of the Carnatic, but was reinstated in 1781. He was twice a member of the British Parliament, became a member of the Supreme Council of Calcutta in 1782, and was Governor General òf India from 1785 to 1786, when he was created a baronet.

Sir Herbert Taylor Macpherson, as a Major-General of the Bengal Staff Corps, served under Havelock at Lucknow, where he gained the V.C. in 1857. He commanded a division in the Afghan War of 1878, was made K.C.B. in 1879, was present at Tel-el-Kebir in 1882, and was Commander-in-Chief at Madras in 1886, when he was sent to organise the pacification of Burma.

A more interesting character than either, however, was Sir Æneas Macpherson, the historian of the clan. Born in 1644, he became successively a writer and advocate, and was Sheriff Depute of Aberdeen in 1684-5. As a Jacobite, after the revolution he suffered imprisonment at home, and afterwards attached himself to the court in exile at St. Germains, where he appears to have been active as a confidential agent. Besides his history of the clan he was the author of various interesting pamphlets and other papers, which were printed by the Scottish History Society in 1902.

Most famous perhaps of all was James Macpherson, the young tutor to Ross of Balnagown, who began by collecting fragments of Gaelic poetry in the Highlands, and published between 1760 and 1764 the famous translations of Ossian, which have given rise to the greatest literary controversy the world has ever seen, and which, whatever their authenticity, played a vital part in the origin of the great Romantic literature which followed their time. As a historian, a pamphleteer, and a civil servant, Macpherson acquired a handsome fortune, and, returning to Scotland, purchased an estate of the old clan lands on the Spey below Kingussie, where he built a fine mansion named Belleville or Balavil. One of his daughters married the famous Sir David Brewster, Principal of Edinburgh University, and their grandson, Mr Charles Julien Brewster-Macpherson, is the owner of Balavil at the present day.

MacPherson Septs

Associated names have a hazy history. Sometimes they had more than one origin; also clouding the precise location of a particular surname might be that name's proscription or of course a migrant population. Even the spelling of surnames was subject to great variations, shifting from usually Latin or Gaelic and heeding rarely to consistent spelling. In early records there can be several spellings of the same name. Undoubtedly contributing to this inconsistency is the handwriting in official records, which was often open to more than one spelling interpretation.

With regard to the 'Mac' prefix, this was, of course, from the Gaelic meaning, son of. It wasn't long before it was abbreviated to 'Mc' or 'M', until we have reached the position now where there are more 'Mc's' than 'Mac's'.

ARCHIBALD From the personal name Archibald, perhaps meaning 'right bold'. Erchenbaldus was the Abbot of Dunfermline in 1180. In 1390 Robert Archebalde had a charter of the Hospital of Roxburgh. Gillespie is considered the Gaelic equivalent of Archibald; the Gillespies being a sept of the Macphersons.

CLARK, CLARKE, CLERK From the occupation of scholar or in earlier times a man in a religious order. Roger Clericus lived in Kelso in 1174. A common name in the Lowlands and found in many old documents throughout Scotland, being a definite surname only after 1400. Claimed by both Clan Chattan and Clan Cameron.

CLARKSON Son of the clerk or scholar. Thomas Clerkson was an interceptor in Aberdeen in 1402. In 1649 Agnes Clerkson was executed for witchcraft in Dirleton, East Lothian.

CURRIE, CURRY From lands of Corrie, now Hutton-Corrie, Dumfriesshire (3 ml E by N of Lockerbie). A form of MacMuirich from Muiriach or Murdoch who was the progenitor of the Macpherson clan.. In 1179 lands in Kyle (Ayrshire) were granted to the Abbey of Melrose by Philip de Curry. In 1342 Walter de Curry was rewarded for playing an important part in capturing Edinburgh castle from the English.

ELLIS, ELLISON From Elias, a common personal name during the middle ages, popularized by the Crusaders. Sept of MacPhersons descended from Elias MacPherson, 1st of Invereshie, who lived in the time of Alexander III. Rogier Elyssonne paid homage in 1296 in Berwick. John Heles was a Dundee burgess in 1482.

GILLESPIE, GILLESPEY, GILISPIE From the Gaelic 'gilleasbuig' the bishop's servant. Sept of the MacPhersons descended from Gillies or Elias MacPherson, younger son of Ewan, ancester of the MacPhersons of Cluny, chiefs of the clan. In 1230 Gillescop of Clavage (near Dunning, SE Perthshire) was witness to a charter concerning lands of Fedale.

GILLIE, GILLIES From the Gaelic 'Gille Iosa' servant of Jesus. A common name in the Hebrides. Patronymic name from Gillies Macpherson who was descended from the chiefs of the clan. In 1128 Gillise was among the witnesses to the charter to the Abbey of Holyrood by King David I. In 1264 Gylis, son of Angus the shoemaker rendered homage at Dull (3 ml W of Aberfeldy).

GOUDIE, GOWDIE, GOW, GOWAN, GOWANS   All these names originate from the Gaelic 'Gow' meaning smith and are descended from Henry of the Wynd, the bandy-legged smith of Perth who fought for the Macphersons at the battle of North Inch of Perth in 1396. The sept are known as 'Sliochd a Ghobha Chrom', race of the bandy-legged smith. Robert Goudie was a writer in Edinburgh in 1643. Henry Gow was a burgess in Dysart in 1580. Colin Gowin Kenvay a known rebel in Tiree in 1675.

LEES   From the Gaelic 'M'Illiosa' son of the gillie of Jesus. The founder of this sept was Gillies or Elias Macpherson, 1st of Invereshie.

MACCLEARY, MACLEAR, MACLEARY   Varient forms of MacChlery from the Gaelic 'M' a'Chleirich', son of the clerk. Claimed by Clan Chattan and Cameron. A profession surname so of common occurence under different clans. Malcolm M'Cleriche took part in an inquest on rights of pasturage in Temple (3 ml SW of Gorebridge station, 7 SW of Dalkeith) in 1461. George Makclearie was a tailor in Edinburgh in 1648.

MACCURRIE, MACCURRY   A form of Macvurich from the Gaelic 'M'Mhuirich' Murdoch who was the progenitor of Clan Macpherson.

MACCURRIE   In 1569 John Mackcurrie was a witness in Dumfries. Murdoch M'Currie was a minister in Saddell in 1639.

MACGOW, MACGOWAN, MACGOUN   From Gaelic 'Macgobhainn' son of the smith. See Gowan. The smith was an important part of the clan as it was he who made the arms and before long the name became a surname. Donald M'Gow paid rent in Drumfallantin (Couper Angus) in 1444. Alister McGhowin was a Royalist in Urray in 1649. (Between Contin and Kilmorack).

MACMURDOCH, MURDOCH   From Gaelic 'Muireach' coming from the sea, a mariner; or 'Murchadh' sea warrior, both names have been confused and intermingled through time. Murdoch was the progenitor of the Macpherson clan. Murdac and Murdoc feature in the Doomsday Book as landowners in Yorkshire, Sussex and Oxfordshire. Murdac was a dean in Appleby, Westmoreland in 1175.

PEARSON, PIERSON   Son of Pierre or Peter. Wautier Pieresone rendered homage in Berwick in 1296. William Piersond was reprieved for the murder of John, Earl of Caithness in 1529. M'A'Phearsain was another way of writing Macpherson and so in time the name merged into Pearson.

SMITH, SMYTH, SMYTHE   A name taken from the occupation of a smith. William the smith took part in an inquest at Traquair in 1274. The name appears on many old documents as Faber or Ferro. The sept of MacPherson named Smith are probably descended from Henry Gow, the bandy-legged smith of Perth. Adam Faber tended a croft in Swaynystoun in 1221-34.   Kenneth, 2nd son of Muirich, progenitor of the Macphersons, was a great artificer in iron and took the name of Smith after his trade.

Clan details in book referred to on facing page

The Suaicheantas, or Badge, is − Lus nam braoileag, red whortle berry bush, *Vaccinium vitis idoea.*

The Cathghairm, "Craig dhu!" the name of a high precipitous rock, over which falls a small stream, and at the base of which are two pretty little lakes called Lochan-uvie.

The Piobaireachdan − The MacPhersons claim "ceann na drochait mòr" as their piobaireachd, alleging that it was composed on occasion of the battle of Perth, fought at "the end of the great bridge" over the Tay, but the Camerons believe that it is theirs. There seems to be a mistake in this for "the end of the *little* bridge," another piece of music. The claim of the composition of one of the pipers, who regretted in the field of battle that he had not three hands, so that he might both fight and play, is not disputed.

The figure is that of a Highland gentleman in full dress. The breacan fheile, or kilt and plaid, of one piece, is of "the grey plaid of Badenach", as worn by Captain Ewen MacPherson, present chief, and twenty-third from Gillichattan mòr. It is, however, somewhat different from the old pattern, which is plainer, and has the colours otherwise arranged. That worn by the clansmen in general as appropriate tartan, is a pretty composition of the red class. In the hose a sett is shown, interesting as having been painted from a plaid woven about two hundred years ago, of remarkably fine texture, the colours still retaining their brilliancy, and it is one of the earliest specimens of hard tartan. The material was spun by one of the ladies of the house of Crubin, represented by Colonel Barkley MacPherson, and it is now in possessionof Mrs Mackintosh, of Stephen's Green, Dublin, to whom she was great great grandmother. It is not considered the common clan tartan, but it has been called the full dress pattern of the chief. The Eideadh ghaelich, or Highland dress, is usually worn by MacMhuraich Chluanadh, and he is one of those who always addresses his countrymen in their mother tongue, the revered language of their fathers.

The McIan illustration of MacPherson published (mid-19th century) in 'The Clans of the Scottish Highlands'

HUGH MACPHERSON

Extract from

KAY'S EDINBURGH PORTRAITS

Hugh MacPherson, or "Wee Hughie", as he was commonly termed, was born in the district of Badenoch, some sixty years ago. When Hughie first ventured forth of his native fastnesses, he made his debut in the Lowlands, attired in the Highland garb – bonnet, kilt, and plaid – with a pair of top-boots in lieu of hose! For some years after his arrival in Perth, he was employed as a clerk in the George Inn; next in the shop of a grocer; and subsequently with Messrs. J. and P. Cameron, carriers betwixt Perth and Edinburgh. The tartans had, long ere this, given way to a coat of dark green, light vest, darkish trousers, and high-heeled boots; a dress to which he adhered without alteration for a length of time. Hughie was, in his own estimation, a perfect dandy. Every new suit, to make sure of being fashionably fitted, cost him a visit to Edinburgh.

Hugh was a well-known character, the oddness of his figure, and his excessive self-conceit, making him the subject of much diversion. While in Perth, some one having drawn a caricature of him, he at once sought reparation by challenging the offender to fight a duel; but this display of spirit only tended to make matters worse, for, in another picture, the little mountaineer was grotesquely exhibited brandishing a pair of pistols not much shorter than himself.

The print of "Little Hughie" was executed in 1810. He had been in Edinburgh a year or two previous.

Some Clan Notables

Macpherson, James *(?-1700)* This illegitimate son of a member of the family of Invershir led a gypsy life. He defiantly evaded magistrates and lairds but was eventually captured. Found guilty of 'going up and doune the country armed and keeping mercats in a hostile manner' he was sentenced to death, although there was no suggestion of blood having been shed on his part'. Prior to his execution he played a dirge on his favourite violin. Reportedly an early version was committed to memory by a female companion of his. Much later it was suggested that Robert Burns' 'Macpherson Farewell' has preserved the original air and lyrics associated with the outlaw's lover.

Macpherson, Paul* *(1756-1846)* Scottish abbe, was born of catholic parents at Scalan on 4 March 1756, and was admitted a student in the seminary there in June 1767, spent two years (1770-2) at the Scots College in Rome, and completed his theological course at the Scots College at Valladolid in Spain. He was sent to Rome in 1793 as agent of the Scottish clergy. General Berthier, by order of the French Directory, took possession of Rome, whereupon Macpherson left the city and travelled through France and England. When the British cabinet was considering the practicability of rescuing Pius VI, then a French prisoner at Savona, on the Genoese coast, an English frigate was ordered to cruise off the land, and Macpherson was despatched from London with ample powers and funds to effect the escape of the pontiff. Spies of the Directory disclosed the design to the Paris government, and the attempt failed. Macpherson was imprisoned, and on his liberation sought refuge in Scotland. On the restoration of Pius VII he returned to Rome once more. The Scots College had been for some time under the control of Italian ecclesiastics, but Macpherson induced the Pope to place the institution under native management, and he was himself appointed its first Scottish record. The first students arrived from Scotland in 1820. He died on 24 November, 1846 in Rome.

Macpherson, William* *(1812-1893),* legal writer, born 19 July 1812, was brother of John Macpherson and of Samuel Charters Macpherson. He was educated at Charterhouse and Trinity College, Cambridge where he graduated B.A. in 1834, and M.A. in 1838. Called to the bar by the Inner Temple in 1837, he published in 1841 a 'Practical Treatise on the Law relating to Infants' which attracted notice owing to its learning and accuracy. In 1846 he went to India to practise at the Indian bar, and in 1848 was given by Sir Laurence Peel, chief-justice of Bengal, the post of master of equity in the supreme court in Calcutta. His 'Procedure of the Civil Courts of India became at once a recognised authority. In December 1861 he had become secretary of the Indian Law Commission, which was appointed to prepare a body of substantive law for India, and he withdrew from literary work in 1867 in order to devote himself solely to that work. The Indian Succession Act of 1865 illustrates the value of the commission's labours, but owing to the Indian government's desire to exercise more direct control over the undertaking, the commission was dissolved in December 1870. Macpherson thereupon returned to the bar, and practised chiefly before the privy council. His useful 'Practice of the Privy Council Judicial Committee,' first published in 1860, reached a second edition in 1873. In 1874 he began reporting the Indian appeals before the privy council for the Council of Law Reporting. In June 1874 he became legal adviser to the India office, and in September 1879 exchanged that post for that of secretary in the judicial department. He retired from the India office 20th February 1882.

Macpherson, John* M.D. *(1817-1890),* physician, younger brother of Samuel Charters Macpherson and son of Hugh Macpherson professor of Greek in the university of Aberdeen, was born at Old Aberdeen in 1817, and after education at the grammar school, entered the university, and there graduated M.A. and was created an honorary M.D. He studied medicine at St. George's Hospital in London, and at a school in Kincerton Street, from 1835 to 1838. He then went abroad, to Bonn, Vienna and Berlin for a year. In October 1839 he became a member of the Royal College of Surgeons of England, and in December sailed for Calcutta as a surgeon in the service of the East

India Company. He held various appointments in Bengal for twenty-four years, and in 1864, having attained the rank of inspector-general of hospitals, returned to England.

Extracts from Dictionary of National Biography, 1899.

Macpherson, Sir David *(1818-1896)* A Highlander who emigrated to Canada eventually becoming a railway contractor. He also successfully contested a parliamentary seat and was appointed to the Senate. His disappointment at not receiving the charter for construction of the Canadian Pacific Railway in competition with a fellow Scot, Sir Hugh Allan, led to a disenchantment with political life. However, he was appointed Speaker of the Senate and minister without portfolio in the Macdonald government.

List of Emigrants assisted by the Highland and Island Emigration Society, and embarked on board the Ship *Priscilla* which sailed from *Liverpool* for *Victoria* on the *13th October* 1852

Name	Age	Residence	Estate	Remarks
McPherson Donald	35	Gramilin	Ditto	£7.19.6 Eligible couple.
Ann	30			
Donald	3			
McPherson Donald	28	Milwaister	Ditto	£18.0.7 Very poor family. Chief support. Well field.
Ann	29	"		
Margaret	5			
Martin	3			
Neil	Infant			
McLeod Peggy	16			
McIntyre John	37	Uig	Ditto	Brother-in-law of McPherson. £20.1.9 Very poor family. —
Mary	32	"		
Arch	13			
Kenneth	11			

Some of the clan emigrants who sailed for Australia